Keep the BIG Things BIG...
and the little things little

Putting things in perspective
and staying positive

Inspired
by Faith

Keep the Big Things Big...and the little things little
ISBN 978-0-9886719-2-8

Published by Product Concept Mfg., Inc.
2175 N. Academy Circle #200, Colorado Springs, CO 80909

©2013 Product Concept Mfg., Inc. All rights reserved.

Written and Compiled by Patricia Mitchell
in association with Product Concept Mfg., Inc.

All scripture quotations are from the King James version
of the Bible unless otherwise noted.

Scriptures taken from the Holy Bible,
New International Version®, NIV®.
Copyright © 1973, 1978, 1984 by Biblica, Inc.™
Used by permission of Zondervan.
All rights reserved worldwide.
www.zondervan.com

Sayings not having a credit listed are contributed by writers
for Product Concept Mfg., Inc. or in a rare case,
the author is unknown.

Keep the
BIG Things BIG...
and the
little things little

Our life is what our thoughts make it.
Marcus Aurelius

It's hard to get perspective

when your eyesight's out of whack! Even one big problem, serious stress, or major worry manages to magnify everything else that comes along, and soon you feel bombarded by a whole lot of really big stuff.

Yes, there are biggies, but few things really qualify. This is a book of stories, reflections, cartoons, quips, and quotes to help you separate all that's big, small, and in-between. It's designed to give you a moment's rest, a few things to think about, and maybe even a chuckle or two. **Keep the Big Things Big...and the little things little** is all about *putting things in perspective and staying positive* through it all!

Perspective Is Everything

In the feast of life, you feel like you've been handed a crust of bread. So *now what?* If you choose, you can take a tip from a toddler and throw the crust on the floor, stomp your feet, and declare you'll starve— just starve!

Or not. Here's a better choice: Scream a little if you need to, but then accept the facts, no matter how difficult. Look at them closely. Choose to highlight in your heart and mind what's good (or at least okay), what's positive, what's encouraging.

You might be surprised to discover that you have a feast in front of you, after all.

Could we change our attitude, we should not only see life differently, but life itself would come to be different.

Katherine Mansfield

Our real blessings often appear to us in the shape of pains, losses and disappointments; but let us have patience, and we soon shall see them in their proper figures.

Joseph Addison

He who has so little knowledge of human nature as to seek happiness by changing anything but his own disposition will waste his life in fruitless efforts.

Samuel Johnson

When life hands you a lemon, you can make lemonade, and…

- Sweeten your sour attitude about lemons.

- Don't associate with people who get you down on lemons.

- Try several of the thousands of fabulous recipes calling for lemon.

- Go visit someone who has a bushel of lemons and ask her how she handles them.

- Extend special understanding to someone who's just gotten a rotten, rotten lemon.

Our Great Big Goals

My friend Jen and I were young, educated, optimistic, and full of great big goals. After graduation, we took on life, determined to get what we wanted, and for a while we succeeded. Then, in the same week, Jen lost her job and my doctor said I had cancer. We cried a lot for days, sometimes out of fear, but mostly out of anger and frustration.

We had plans! How could this be happening to us?

Not until years later did I realize the importance of how you see things, especially when things go wrong. Jen, a normally sunny, happy sort of gal, dried her tears and charted a new career path for herself. It eventually worked into her own small business: a business she loves.

   Me, I'm not generally optimistic, but I learned to be after I met so many sick people who had given up on themselves. I didn't want to be like them. Sure, it took me months to get into the habit of being thankful every day, but my new attitude took me through some really tough patches. And now I'm convinced that a good attitude, no matter what happens, is the greatest and biggest goal anyone could have.

Travel with your eyes. Let them look at you where you are, and let your vision stretch to the furthest horizon. Survey a landscape of hills and valleys, deserts and forests, majestic seas and trickling brooks. Recognize great vistas and hidden pathways…hear the songs of summer's dancing wildflowers and the still, soft silence of newly fallen snow.

Come back refreshed. Come back home with a new perspective on every time, place, and season. Breathe deeply. Take courage. Envision a world where everything rests in the sight of a loving and compassionate God.

To every thing there is a season, and a time to every purpose under the heaven.

Ecclesiastes 3:1

Sunshine is delicious, rain is refreshing,
wind braces up, snow is exhilarating;
there is really no such thing as bad weather,
only different kinds of good weather.

John Ruskin

Here's What Ya Oughta Do...

"Just let go and flap your arms.
It's a cinch. Trust me."

Don't you just love advice?

Sooo helpful! But you grin and bear it because you know your mother/friend/co-worker means well and is really trying to help.

Most advice makes it sound as if everything is easy and simple, and you're the one who insists on making things difficult. And let's face it—easy and simple might be how your problem looks to outsiders. Only you know the depths of your emotions and the number of hidden hurdles you might be facing.

So you see a big problem and someone else sees a small problem. Maybe…just maybe… the truth lies somewhere in the middle.

So true...

- Anyone can give advice—the trick is in finding someone interested in taking it.

- The best way to succeed in life is to act on the advice we give to other people.

- The best time to give advice to your children is while they're still young enough to believe you know what you're talking about.

- She who builds on everyone's advice will soon have a crooked house.

Money Matters

At 21 and just out of college, Meg was delighted to land her first job and get her own apartment. But a month later, she returned home in tears. "Dad!" she wailed, "what you told me about money wasn't true at all!"

"What do you mean?" her dad exclaimed.

"You told me to put my money in the bank on Main Street," she said, "and now it's insolvent!"

Dad was flabbergasted. "Ridiculous! That's the biggest and the most solid bank in the state!"

"No, it isn't," she wailed. "I just got one of my checks back with a note saying Insufficient Funds!"

OK, let's get serious – good counsel and wise advice from others helps immeasurably. From those who have lived long and thoughtfully, we can learn how to avoid common pitfalls and make the most of life. Often friends and family members can see an angle we can't, and their insight expands our vision and understanding. Perhaps a chapter in their life's story can bring us the perspective we so desperately need.

When it comes to advice, all we have to do is listen…and, if it's good advice, it's good to take it!

Advice is like castor oil, easy enough to give but dreadful uneasy to take.
Josh Billings

Nobody can give you wiser advice than yourself.
Cicero

I give myself sometimes admirable advice, but I am incapable of taking it.
Mary Wortley Montagu

It is easy when we are in prosperity to give advice to the afflicted.
Aeschylus

It's a matter of choosing…

- The best way over the most convenient way.

- Wise words over shallow platitudes.

- Serene thoughts over stormy emotions.

- Trust in God over reliance on yourself.

Lord, there's nothing in this world
that you and I can't handle together.

Whatever you do, you need courage.
Whatever course you decide upon,
there is always someone to tell you
that you are wrong.
There are always difficulties arising
that tempt you to believe your critics are right.
To map out a course of action and follow it to an end
requires some of the same courage that a soldier needs.
Peace has its victories,
but it takes brave men and women to win them.

Ralph Waldo Emerson

Not to Worry!

"Mama said there'd be days like this."

Not a day goes by without another trauma! That's the way it feels, anyway, when life gets out of balance. Instead of noting that plenty of things are going well—or at least continuing on quietly and unobtrusively—our inner trauma queen fixes her royal gaze on one blip on the radar. In the space of an hour, the blip morphs into an asteroid heading straight this way.

A balanced life fixes one eye on the blip (you know, it just might be an asteroid after all) and the other eye on all the small, wonderful, miraculous blips—the joys, blessings, and daily pleasures that are ours for the taking.

Do not anticipate trouble or worry about what may never happen. Keep in the sunlight.

Benjamin Franklin

Needless fear and panic over disease or misfortune that seldom materialize are simply bad habits. By proper ventilation and illumination of the mind, it is possible to cultivate tolerance, poise and real courage.

Elie Metchnikoff

Whatsoever things are true, whatsoever things are honest, whatsoever things are just, whatsoever things are pure, whatsoever things are lovely, whatsoever things are of good report…think on these things.

Philippians 4:8

We ease our own troubles when
we help someone else with theirs. All it takes
is a warm smile to light a gloomy face…
a friendly word to lift a heavy heart…
a listening ear to chase away loneliness and
fear. With a heartfelt prayer for a friend who
is ill…a thoughtful gift for a relative who
grieves…a selfless donation to help those who
have so much less…somehow our own worries
drift away to nothingness.

Drag your thoughts away from your troubles…
by the ears, by the heels,
or any other way you can manage it.

Mark Twain

Okay, it is an asteroid, *but...*

- It isn't the worst that could have happened, so you have a reason to give thanks.

- You've worked through other problems, so you've got what it takes to work through this one.

- Others have faced similar circumstances, so there's help and support available... just ask.

- It's happened, so now you can focus on what to do about it.

- Good often comes out of bad, so there's reason for hope and acceptance.

- God knows about it, so you can turn to Him for comfort and understanding, help and strength.

Time Tested

I woke up late, and the worry machine switched on. Would I get to work on time? Would my boss see me come in late? Would I be able to finish the project I was working on by the end of the afternoon? What about getting home in time to attend my son's soccer game? Before I had even gotten out of bed, my stomach was in knots!

But a still, small voice inside me said, "Stop." Almost involuntarily, I stopped. My heart filled with thanksgiving for being able to step out of bed…for my darling son asleep in the next room…for the clothes we would wear that day and the breakfast we would eat…for the job I have and the school he attends.

That day, I didn't hurry and I didn't rush. The most important things got done, and I was more than satisfied.

All's Well

Two pigeons agreed that they would meet for a date on the ledge outside the ninth floor of an office building. The gal pigeon was at the appointed place right on time, but her guy was nowhere in sight. As the minutes passed, she became increasingly distraught, imagining all the horrible things that could have happened to her friend.

Half an hour later, her guy appeared on the ledge. Breathing a sigh of relief, she asked him where he had been all this time.

"Oh, it was such a nice day," the guy pigeon answered, "so I decided to walk."

No longer forward nor behind
I look in hope and fear;
But grateful take the good I find,
The best of now and here.
John Greenleaf Whittier

Human Resources

A true friend always has your back!

People who love and care about you want to help, and they come to your rescue in countless ways. When you're burdened, they provide extra hands to lighten your load. When you need someone to talk to, they are the ones who take the time to hear you out. When you simply want to know that someone's there…they are.

It's easy to think that they don't understand, but friends and family are the ones who know you best. They're the ones most likely to know where you're coming from and to help you keep going forward. They're the ones you can depend on to have your back when you're facing tough and challenging times.

On the Prairie

Out on the lone prairie, several buffalo were grazing when a surly cowboy rode up alongside them. He stopped his horse and glared at them for several minutes. Then he spat on the ground. "You want to know my opinion?" he said. "I think you're the ugliest critters I've ever seen." With that, the cowboy turned and rode off.

One buffalo languidly turned to his companions and said, "Fellas, I think we just heard a discouraging word."

And the buffalo nodded in agreement and kept on grazing quietly and contentedly.

Friendship is a sheltering tree.
Samuel Taylor Coleridge

My only sketch, profile, of heaven
is a large blue sky, and larger than the
biggest I have seen in June—and in it
are my friends—every one of them.
Emily Dickinson

Of all the things which wisdom
provides to make life entirely happy,
much the greatest is the possession
of friendship.
Epicurus

Some people don't lighten our load, they make it heavier. A judgmental family member, a bossy friend, a nitpicking coworker are difficult people who can cause overwhelming stress in our life. Negative remarks undermine our ability to stay positive. Bullying behavior seizes control over our emotions. Unjustified demands sap our energy and rob us of the time we need for renewal and relaxation.

While we may not be able to avoid difficult people completely, we can do something about the stress they cause.

5 R's for coping with difficult people...

- **R**emain in control of your emotions. Use specific situations and non-threatening words to describe what the person does that you would like him or her to change. Politely and privately discuss with the person a good solution.

- **R**esolve to not let the difficult person's behavior bother you; remember, the problem is with them, not with you.

- **R**efuse to take offense at what people say to you, and never trade insult for insult, argument for argument. Instead, forgive.

- **R**espond compassionately; pay truthful compliments; you never know what someone has suffered in the past or is suffering now.

- **R**espect the difficult person, despite everything. He or she—just like you—is a son or daughter of God, creator of all.

5 C's for nurturing wonderful people...

- **C**reate time for those who mean the most to you…they're the ones who keep you centered, balanced, positive about life and spiritually rejuvenated.

- **C**ommunicate frequently, even if it's a short card, note, or email to say, "I'm thinking of you today."

- **C**hoose to forgive; never let a misunderstanding or resentment fester between you.

- **C**onfide in those you love—they care about you; and keep their confidences to you confidential.

- **C**oncentrate on them alone when they're with you…there's nothing more important.

Sometimes we find a best friend
right in our own family.

Oh, the comfort, the inexpressible comfort
of feeling safe with a person,
having neither to weigh thoughts nor measure words,
but pouring them all out, just as they are,
chaff and grain together,
certain that a faithful hand will take and sift them,
keep what is worth keeping,
and with a breath of kindness blow the rest away.

Dinah Maria Mulock Craik

A Dose of Laughter

"I feel better already!"

Laughter is good for you!

It's a time-honored and highly recommended medicine to soothe a hurting soul, lift a saddened heart—and get things back in perspective.

A good belly laugh—or even a heart-tickling chuckle—is a healthy reminder not to take things (and ourselves) so seriously. It lightens our mood, relieves frustration, and shifts our thinking into a more positive mode. For life balance and a healthy perspective, humor is just what the doctor ordered!

No, laughter might not be the cure, but it sure makes you feel a whole lot better!

Laughter...

See it in the dance of sunbeams over water,
Hear it in the shouts of kids at play…
Find it in the smile you give a lonely stranger,
Sense it in the newness of each day.

Laughter...

Notice it in all your burdens, griefs, and sorrows...
Open to its calming, soothing grace.
Call and let the sparkling light of laughter answer
Here and now, and in this time and place.

Fresh Perspective

Three restaurants opened on the same block. The owner of the first eatery put up a sign claiming "Best Restaurant in the City!" The owner of the second put up a larger sign declaring "Best Restaurant in the World!"

The owner of the third stood outside and looked at the two signs. The next morning a sign appeared on the front of his establishment:

Best Restaurant on This Block

He that is of a merry heart hath a continual feast.

Proverbs 15:15

Laughter is the sun that drives winter from the human face.

Victor Hugo

We are all here for a spell; get all the good laughs you can.

Will Rogers

A person without a sense of humor is like a wagon without springs—jolted by every pebble in the road.

Henry Ward Beecher

Decide to laugh...

- Hang out with people who see the humorous side of life.

- Watch your favorite comedian or funny movie; listen to entertaining pop songs; read a lighthearted book.

- Do something silly...skip instead of walk... wear a goofy hat... do the hokey-pokey... whistle while you work.

- Spend less time with negative news and dire predictions, and more time with friends, kids, and cuddly animals.

- Open your arms. Smile. Say Yes to life.

Laugh, and the world laughs with you;
Weep, and you weep alone.
For the sad old earth must borrow its mirth,
But has trouble enough of its own.
Sing, and the hills will answer;
Sigh, it is lost on the air.
The echoes bound to a joyful sound,
But shrink from voicing care.

Ella Wheeler Wilcox

Whatever Is...Is

"Hey, gimme five...or one, or whatever..."

"Whatever." Though typically accompanied by a teen's lackadaisical shrug, when we say it with a smile, "Whatever!" reveals an attitude of trust and confidence. Only someone who trusts in God and in His unchanging loving kindness can happily say "Whatever!" and mean it—whatever life brings, it's OK. Whatever happens, it's manageable.

"Whatever" is true for you. Whatever is going on today and whatever tomorrow brings is something you can handle. It's God-given. It's within you. It's yours.

Whatever Works

Dad, frustrated by his teen's lackadaisical attitude toward his homework and household chores, complained to one of his coworkers. "When I was his age," Dad said, "my father would send me to my room for a couple hours' time out. But in my son's room, there's a TV, computer, games console, cell phone, and CD player."

"So what do you do?" asked the coworker.

"I do what works," Dad replied. "I send him to my room."

Happy the man who early learns the wide chasm that lies between his wishes and his powers.

Johann Wolfgang von Goethe

Be willing to have it so. Acceptance of what has happened is the first step to overcoming the consequences of any misfortune.

William James

The reasonable man adapts himself to the world; the unreasonable one persists in trying to adapt the world to himself.

George Bernard Shaw

I make the most of all that comes and the least of all that goes.

Sara Teasdale

Acceptance isn't resignation.

Rather, it's an honest recognition that there are some things we cannot change. They lie out of our control. So rather than rail against them, why not confront them? Rather than ignore them as if it will go away, it's better to say, "So this is so; how might I respond?"

Identify the hindrance, and then do what other resolute people have done before you—work over it, around it, through it. Do anything but imagine it negatively defines your failure. Instead, let it ignite new ideas, fresh solutions. Let it positively define your courage and perseverance.

Acceptance means...

- You aren't astonished because things haven't turned out the way you expected or anticipated or would have preferred. Surprises happen, and life goes on.

- You can think back to times when loss or catastrophe turned into the start of growth, rejuvenation, and unforeseen opportunities.

- You look into the various aspects of what's happening and what it may (or may not) mean to you. Doing so gives you control over your feelings and your response.

- You've learned to relax and watch what life brings. You've come this far, and there's no reason to think you won't keep going a lot further!

Aesop's Fable of the Reed and the Oak

A giant oak and a tender reed were arguing about their relative strength and longevity. Just as the great tree began to laugh at the pretentions of the lowly reed, a great gust of wind came up and ripped across the land. Darkness came, and night fell. The next morning, the sun arose upon a tranquil landscape and looked upon all that taken place.

The sun saw that the oak, which had stubbornly fought against the great wind, lay on the ground, uprooted. The reed, which in its meekness and humility bent to the wind, stood tall, flourishing in the morning light.

When we see ourselves in a situation
which must be endured and gone through,
it is best to meet it with firmness,
and accommodate everything to it
in the best way practicable.
This lessens the evil,
while fretting and fuming
only increase your own torments.

Thomas Jefferson

The Power of "No"

"I wish I could, but Mom says I can't come
out and play with you...ever."

Positively no! It sounds like an oxymoron—what's "positive" about an emphatic "no," after all? But when you think about it, an emphatic "no" has the power to create some very positive changes in our life.

All it takes is a simple, well-directed "no" to free you from no-longer-fun activities that eat up your evenings and weekends. "No" gets you, not other people, in control of how you'll spend your time, money, and energy. "No" puts an end to what you've always done...so you can begin what you'd like to do *now*.

How to nicely say "No"...

- Assess what you want to do and your available time before accepting invitations.

- Keep it simple. Your "other plans," whatever they may be, need no explanation.

- Remain firm. If you waver, or start giving excuses, your "no" easily morphs into "maybe."

- Suggest new ways of doing things. Holiday get-togethers, for example, might prove more enjoyable at another, less stressful, time of year.

To know what you prefer, instead of humbly saying "Amen" to what the world tells you you ought to prefer, is to keep your soul alive.

Robert Louis Stevenson

Seek out that particular mental attitude which makes you feel most deeply and vitally alive, along with which comes the inner voice which says, "This is the real me," and when you have found that attitude, follow it.

William James

Remember always that you have not only the right to be an individual, you have an obligation to be one.

Eleanor Roosevelt

Choose always the way that seems the best, however rough it may be; custom will soon render it easy and agreeable.

Pythagoras

Don't neglect yourself...

even if you've said "yes" to too many things right now, you still need to laugh with friends, look up at the stars, do something you love, and take time out just for you. Only a firm but gentle "no" will allow you a moment's personal space.

Might others become irritated or be inconvenienced? Perhaps, especially if they're accustomed to hearing you say "yes," no matter what else you may have planned or would prefer to do. Ultimately, however, their feelings are their responsibility. After all, no matter what you do, someone isn't going to be pleased...so you may as well please yourself!

I've Got Plans

Three mice were sitting around bragging about their strength, bravery, and prowess. The first mouse stood up and said, "Mouse traps? Pfft! They're nothing to me. In fact, I do push-ups with the bar while eating the cheese!"

The second mouse lazily reached inside his pocket and pulled out a capsule. "See this, guys?" He popped the pill into his mouth and swallowed it. "That was rat poison. I eat it for a snack."

The third mouse got up and headed for the door. "Hey, where do you think you're going?" the other two mice hollered.

"Time to get home," the third mouse said. "I haven't chased the cat yet today."

When not to say "No"…

- When you genuinely want to do it.

- When it's meaningful, memory-making, and rewarding to you.

- When you believe you will later regret not doing it.

- When your heart says "yes."

Have regular hours for work and play;
make each day both useful and pleasant,
and prove that you understand the worth of time
by employing it well. Then youth will be delightful,
old age will bring few regrets,
and life will become a beautiful success.

Louisa May Alcott

Pick What You Love

"Hey, honk if you love squirrels!!"

Opportunities abound! Actually, so many opportunities abound that most of us grab too many of them. Yes, we can learn another language, play another musical instrument, buy season tickets to several events, get another academic degree, take up another hobby…but probably not all at one time. When we attempt to do too much, life gets frantic and we're unlikely to enjoy what we're doing, or do anything well.

"Honk" if you love it…but if you're looking for a positive, fulfilling experience—and a sane schedule—think twice before adding it to your calendar!

Diminishing Returns

Every Sunday afternoon, my mom and dad and I went to an all-you-can-eat restaurant. The sight of a dozen or so desserts at the end of the buffet set my mouth watering every time, and I always begged for several instead of just one. One time, my dad gave in and told me I could take whatever I wanted, as much as I wanted. I was ecstatic!

I blissfully gobbled up a slice of chocolate cake, a bowl of apple cobbler, a dish of ice cream, and two chocolate chip cookies. As we got up to leave, though, I realized I didn't feel so well and I held my hands to my tummy.

"Too much of a good thing isn't very good, is it?" my dad said. It was his way of teaching me the law of diminishing returns, and I've remembered the lesson to this day.

People can have many different kinds
of pleasure. The real one is that for
which they will forsake the others.
Marcel Proust

What do you want most to do?
That's what I have to keep asking myself.
Katherine Mansfield

One cannot manage too many affairs:
like pumpkins in the water, one pops up
while you try to hold down the other.
Proverb

Even if you love everything...

- Choose between conflicting activities or goals, even if both are desirable; pick the one that's most important to you.

- Consider your present responsibilities, available time, and stage in life before taking on a new opportunity.

- Determine your long-term goals; avoid anything that would hinder them.

- Encourage the efforts of those involved in activities you support, but cannot experience right now. Be their appreciative audience!

From a spiritual perspective, the most important thing in life is who you are on the inside. Feelings of self-worth, fulfillment, and life balance are affected by what we're doing and the choices we make, but start with peace within yourself and with God.

A spiritual perspective puts problems, activities, worries, and concerns in their place, and lets you focus on genuine goals and important topics. Knowing your life's purpose is essential for picking what's significant in your life and for choosing what you will support, embrace, and do.

Never undertake anything
for which you wouldn't have the courage
to ask the blessings of heaven.
Georg Christoph Lichtenberg

Knowledge of what is possible is
the beginning of happiness.

George Santayana

What seemed easy in imagination
was rather hard in reality.

Lucy Maud Montgomery

Happy the man who early learns the
wide chasm that lies between his
wishes and his powers.

Johann Wolfgang von Goethe

Half the unhappiness in the world is due
to the failure of plans which were never
reasonable, and often impossible.

Edgar Watson Howe

What an immense power over the life
is the power of possessing distinct aims.
The voice, the dress, the look,
the very motions of a person,
define and alter when he or she begins
to live for a reason.

Elizabeth Stuart Phelps

Daily Blessings

**Sometimes it's the little things
that mean the most.**

We remember the big things—
both the happy ones and the not-so-happy ones. Those events and experiences of yesterday shine brightly in our mind, often overshadowing what's going on today.

Perhaps today holds no momentous, memory-making events. One thing's for sure, though. We miss an abundance of little joys, daily blessings, and tender gifts when we measure today by any other day, past or future.

Sure, the biggies are part of our life's story, but sometimes it's the little things that mean the most.

Most of the shadows of this life are caused by standing in one's own sunshine.

Ralph Waldo Emerson

There shall be showers of blessing.

Ezekiel 34:26

Is it so small a thing to have enjoy'd the sun, to have lived light in the spring, to have loved, to have thought, to have done?

Matthew Arnold

The mere sense of living is joy enough.

Emily Dickinson

Little Lesson

A mother mouse and her little one were strolling in the sunshine when suddenly the neighborhood tomcat sprang in front of them and snarled. Mom mouse stopped, stood as tall as she could, and bellowed, "Woof! Woof! Woof!" The stunned tom turned tail and scampered away.

"See?" Mom said to her little one as they continued their walk. "That's why it's so important to learn a second language!"

Of Weeds and Seeds

"Cherish the blossoms"—it's something my grandmother told me. When I was small, I wanted to help her pull weeds in her flower garden. Before trusting me with my own trowel, though, she carefully showed me the difference between invading weeds and sprouting seeds. She kept an eagle eye on me until she was convinced I had learned my lesson well!

When I had my own home, I planted a flower garden. Then I got too busy to take care of it. In no time, weeds took over, choking out most of the tender seedlings I had so carefully tucked in the ground. Now it would take hours and hours of work to rid my garden of the weeds. Sigh!

As I knelt down, trowel in hand, to start digging, it occurred to me that our troubles are a lot like weeds. Faced when they're small, they don't get a chance to take over and choke out all the good things in life—the tender sprouts, the beautiful blossoms.

Now I cherish the "blossoms" in my life by getting problems out in the open as soon as they show up so I can weed them out. If there's a misunderstanding with someone, I'm the first to talk about it so it won't grow into a huge issue later on. It's the kind of weeding that keeps life's difficulties small and its blossoms big every day.

Five ways to weed out problems when they're small...

- Define the problem in accurate and unemotional terms so you know precisely what the issue is.

- Share the problem only with those who are involved, or who have the skill, knowledge, or expertise to help you solve it.

- Avoid quick conclusions; think analytically and creatively to reach a logical and effective solution.

- Implement the solution with conviction and persistence. A change of habit, attitude, or expectations takes time!

- Evaluate the effectiveness of your solution. If it's not working after an appropriate time, try another approach.

The best things are nearest:
breath in your nostrils, light in your eyes,
flowers at your feet, duties at your hand,
the path of God just before you.
Then do not grasp at the stars,
but do life's plain, common work as it comes
certain that daily duties and daily bread
are the sweetest things of life.

Robert Louis Stevenson

Cheer Up!

"Hey, come on, can't you quack a smile?"

Imagining the best outcome in harmony with the truth. Unfortunately, we all have a tendency to dwell on the worst that could happen in any given circumstance. Expect the best!

Cherishing others. Everyone—even the frailest of body and mind—is a beloved child of God. Treat others not necessarily on account of who they are, but Whose they are.

Encouraging others to see the bright side of life. Laugh with them, listen to their life's story, give the warmth of genuine love and compassion.

Why you serve others...

- You've had your share of problems, and you know how it feels.

- You've been helped through tough times, and now you want to pass it on.

- You've found that helping others reduces stress by getting your mind off your own troubles.

- You feel more positive about life when you reach out to others.

- You believe it's the right thing to do...and besides, it makes you feel really good!

Volunteering for an organization is a great way to help people! You get not only the thanks of those in need, but you meet other volunteers who share your goals and values. Sounds like a good place to make new friends or meet someone special, doesn't it?

Most churches encourage their members to visit shut-ins, bring food to needy or grieving families, organize food and clothing drives, and lead activities for children and teens. Many non-profit agencies need extra people over the holidays, and that's a way to get a taste of volunteering before making a long-term commitment. Or just say, "I'm here to give this a try. What do you want me to do?"

At the heart of life is service.
Mother Teresa

A man wrapped up in himself makes a very small bundle.

Benjamin Franklin

The best way to cheer yourself up is to try to cheer somebody else up.

Mark Twain

What do we live for, if not to make life less difficult for each other?

George Eliot

The true way to soften one's troubles is to solace those of others.

Madame de Maintenon

I expect to pass through this world but once.
Any good therefore that I can do,
or any kindness or abilities that I can show
to any fellow creature, let me do it now.
Let me not defer it or neglect it,
for I shall not pass this way again.

William Penn

Do You Hear Me?

"Hey, I'm all ears!"

Do you like to lend an ear? If so, you probably don't realize how many times you've blessed the day for others. Just think about how good you feel when someone really hears what you're saying!

It doesn't matter whether you're confiding in your best friend or exchanging casual greetings with the person ringing up your groceries—you know when you're being heard. There's a welcoming smile, eye-to-eye contact, and a meaningful response. There's connection, and connection feels good.

Sure, listening isn't always convenient. Yet the few minutes you take to really hear what someone else is saying just might be the high point in that person's day.

The greatest compliment that was ever paid me was when one asked me what I thought, and attended to my answer.
Henry David Thoreau

To listen closely and reply well is the highest perfection we are able to attain in the art of conversation.
François de La Rochefoucauld

There are people who, instead of listening to what is being said to them, are already listening to what they are going to say themselves.
Albert Guinon

Tactful Answer

At a family gathering, an elderly aunt asked her young nephew to guess her age. He hesitated to answer, so she said with a teasing smile, "You have some idea how old I am, don't you?"

"Well, yes, I do," the nephew replied, "but I don't know whether to make it ten years younger because of your appearance, or ten years older because of your intelligence."

Listen...

- Give your full attention to the person who's facing you. That means everything else is less important right now, including the demands of electronic devices and the entrance of someone else you'd rather talk to.

- Grasp not just the words, but the emotion behind the words. Sometimes the real message lies hidden in voice tone, facial expression, and body language.

- Show respect, even if you don't agree with what the person is saying, or you think it's a trivial matter. Your opinion will be dismissed if the person feels judged or belittled.

- Pause before responding, even if there's a gap in the conversation. This way you won't be tempted to compose your answer while someone else is talking.

- Learn about controversial issues by listening to people affected, to those who have knowledge of the matter, and to those with points of view unlike your own.

- Listen not only with your ears, but with your head and heart. Bring your thoughts, feelings, knowledge, and humanity to the conversation.

- Reveal that you understand what someone else has said by asking thoughtful and relevant questions; and by making meaningful comments.

- Open yourself to others. You know how you feel when someone listens to you… do the same for the people you meet every day. The good feelings you spread to others will surely bounce back to you!

The Wise Old Owl

A wise old owl sat on an oak—
The more he saw, the less he spoke.
The less he spoke, the more he heard.
Why aren't we like that wise old bird?

Speak, LORD; for thy servant heareth.
1 Samuel 3:9

It is the province of knowledge to speak
and it is the privilege of wisdom to listen.
Oliver Wendell Holmes

Know how to listen, and you will profit
even from those who talk badly.
Plutarch

If speaking is silver, then listening is gold.
Proverb

A good listener is not only popular
everywhere, but after a while he
knows something.
Wilson Mizner

I'm Sorry

**"It would be really big of you,
but can you forgive me–a little?"**

***Forgiveness isn't always easy*—** but without a willingness to forgive, hurt feelings fester and old wounds never heal. You probably know how it goes: Where there's no forgiveness, a minor misunderstanding bursts into a major fight. When no one has the spunk to offer an apology or the grace to accept one, relationships rip apart.

A timely "I'm sorry" soothes hurt feelings, lessens pain, and keeps the offense from exploding out of proportion. A sincere apology, even a belated one, can put a remorseful heart at rest and bring peace to a wounded soul.

Forgiveness is like a salve. It soothes burning wounds of the heart and promotes healing and wellness. Like suture, it brings together what has been torn apart.

Forgiveness is like an open door. It releases anger and bitterness and welcomes respect, understanding, and tolerance. Like a welcoming smile, it is an act of generosity that promises reconciliation, friendship, and love.

Forgiveness is like a bridge. It links two sides and makes it possible to pass over the chasm of offense and disappointment, injury and betrayal. It spans the valley of vengeance and lifts a willing heart above the abyss of hostility.

Forgiveness is like the contented purr of a cuddly kitten or the joyful warmth of a velvety pup. It forgets the past, celebrates growth, and goes forward to live, laugh, and love again.

Life appears to me too short to be spent
in nursing animosity or registering wrongs.

Charlotte Brontë

Never does the human soul appear so
strong as when it foregoes revenge and
dares to forgive an injury.

Edwin Hubbell Chapin

He who forgives ends the quarrel.

Proverb

If you forgive men when they sin
against you, your heavenly Father
will also forgive you.

Matthew 6:14 NIV

Hatred is like fire—it makes even light
rubbish deadly.

George Eliot

Forgiveness and Friendship

We laugh about it now, but at the time it tore our friendship apart. Working at the same company, Amy and I became best friends. We gabbed at lunch, went out in the evening, and even took weekend road trips together. Then Brendon joined the company. He was cute, personable, and fun to be around. He and Amy hit it off right away and began dating.

A short time later, I started meeting Brendon on the sly, even though I knew Amy was getting serious about him. It didn't take long before she found out, and she was furious! She had been betrayed by two people she trusted. She stopped speaking to both of us.

I continued seeing Brendon but I missed Amy terribly. This went on for several months. Then I heard about Ginger.

Ginger worked for another company, but a gal in my department knew her. With a snarky smile, she let me (and everyone else) know that Brendon and Ginger were an item and had been for quite a while. My pride plunged to the basement. I left early that day, saying I wasn't feeling well. No lie, because I was miserable.

That day, I called Amy and asked if we could talk. All I wanted to tell her was that I had been a jerk, and I was sorry I had betrayed her. I didn't expect her to forgive me…but she did. I was blessed by the grace she extended to me. We went out for a wickedly good dessert to celebrate a difficult lesson learned…and a wonderful friendship restored.

Forgiving ways...

- Think about the harm lack of forgiveness does to your own peace of mind. There are few things more upsetting, stressful, and anxiety-ridden than nursing a hurt or bearing a grudge.

- Consider the other person's point of view. Both of you might feel the other is at fault and should make the first move.

- Let go of resentment, even if the person has done considerable harm to you. Resentment eats away at you, not the other person.

- Decide that, no matter who's at fault, you will forgive the other person, whether or not you can or want to continue the relationship.

When you go to bed at night,
have for your pillow three things—
love, hope and forgiveness.
And you will awaken in the morning
with a song in your heart.

Victor Hugo

What's It Look Like?

"Are horseflies getting better looking,
or am I just terribly lonely?"

Say the boss plops a project on your desk and expects you to get it done ASAP. Suppose your sis drops by with her kids in tow, hoping you'll watch them for a few hours while she goes to an appointment. Imagine a friend calling you up and asking for a huge favor.

If you're feeling good and have nothing else planned, there's no problem. You're happy to do it. But if you aren't feeling so good and there's a lot on your mind, there's a big problem. And you're pretty steamed about it, too.

What things look like depends a lot on how you're feeling.

Everything poses a problem when...

- You're tired or not feeling well, but you're determined to keep on keeping on.

- You have pressing problems to deal with, and they're all closing in on you at once.

- You have too much to do in too little time; you're running from one place to the next, from one activity to the other.

- You don't like things the way they are, so anything that comes along is an occasion of irritation or outright hostility.

Some things that might help...

• Make rest and wellness a priority. You're no good to anyone if you're tired, and fatigue makes you more susceptible to stress and illness.

• Define the issues you're confronting—rank them according to urgency and importance, and then tackle one at a time.

• Scrutinize your schedule for anything you can delegate, minimize, or eliminate. Be realistic about what you can do on any given day.

• Take responsibility for your attitude. Cultivate thankfulness, enjoyment, and the privilege of being alive. Choose to change.

What we see depends mainly on what we look for.

John Lubbock

What concerns me is not the way things are, but rather the way people think things are.

Epictetus

Believe that life is worth living, and your belief will help create the fact.

William James

The fault-finder will find faults even in paradise.

Henry David Thoreau

Our thoughts determine our reality. Imagine, if you will, a child whose parents have showered on him all a kid could wish for—electronics, games, books, sports equipment, and a closetful of trendy clothes. But if he's a sullen, discontented sort, he'll find something wrong with everything he's been given. Not one thing looks good to him.

Now let's plant a contented and thankful heart into this kid, and voilà! Same scene, but a totally different reaction. He likes what he sees. Everything is a blessing. And it's easy to think he'd be just as excited with only one of his generous parents' gifts!

People only see what they are prepared to see.

Ralph Waldo Emerson

How She Sees It

One day a woodpecker was pecking a hole in a large oak tree. Suddenly the sky darkened, the winds came up, and a streak of lightning sent the oak toppling to the ground.

"Wow!" exclaimed the astonished woodpecker. Thoroughly impressed with herself, she declared, "I guess I don't know my own strength!"

The world is a looking-glass
and gives back to every man the reflection
of his own face. Frown at it and it will in
turn look sourly upon you;
laugh at it and with it, and it is a jolly,
kind companion.

William Makepeace Thackeray

Safe Landing

Things are a little up in the air right now.

As if we were leaves in a whirlwind, unresolved issues, ongoing challenges, and troubling problems keep us spinning. Everything's up in the air—and so are we! Not a good feeling, is it? But even on calm and sunny days, we can't predict what tomorrow will bring—it's just that crises have a way of bringing us face-to-face with the fact.

Another fact is God's presence in the middle of your whirlwind. He knows the outcome. Hold on to His steady hand, and rest assured you'll land on your feet again.

I will never leave thee, nor forsake thee.

Hebrews 13:5

God gives us always strength enough,
and sense enough, for everything He
wants us to do.

John Ruskin

There are moments when, whatever be
the attitude of the body, the soul is on
its knees.

Victor Hugo

Act boldly and unseen forces will come
to your aid.

Dorothea Brande

The Power Within

Two terrified skunks were running as fast as they could to get away from a dog that was chasing them through the forest. When they came upon a third skunk, they yelled, "Quick! Run! Hound's after us!"

"Calm down, fellas, calm down," the third skunk told them. As the other two looked at him in amazement, he bowed his head and said, "Let us spray."

Unsettled times, for many of us, bring anxiety and fear. But for some, the best time to branch out, try new things, and explore viable directions is when everything's up in the air. Dislodged from our familiar foundation, we discover personal strengths and unexpected opportunities unimaginable with feet firmly—and safely—planted on the ground.

You may have to take a risk and do something you've never done before. Great! Even if you stumble, you will have gained experience—experience you can get in no other way except to step out into the unknown.

Even if you're on the right track, you'll get run over if you just sit there.
Will Rogers

How to get moving when everything's moving around you…

- Go forward; don't struggle to get things back the way they were. Things have changed, and so can you.

- Use the opportunity to broaden your perspective, deepen your faith, and experience another aspect of life.

- Do your homework and take smart—not rash or reckless—risks.

- Put your trust in God; pray, and then act.

Uncertainty and expectation are the joys of life. Security is an insipid thing.

William Congreve

Without risk, faith is an impossibility.

Søren Kierkegaard

However well organized the foundation of life may be, life must always be full of risks.

Havelock Ellis

The fishermen know that the sea is dangerous and the storm terrible, but they have never found these dangers sufficient reason for remaining ashore.

Vincent van Gogh

Be like the bird that,
passing on her flight awhile
on boughs too slight,
feels them give way beneath her,
and yet sings,
knowing that she hath wings.

Victor Hugo

What's Up With This?

"Sure, I like to play fetch...
but this is ridiculous!"

What's going on? That's not always an easy question to answer. Sure, you know what the topic is, but it's sort of like knowing the plot of a book you've never read. You know the subject, but not the details. You can name the main characters, but you don't know who else figures into the story.

Sometimes you simply don't have all the information, but you have to make a decision anyway. So base your decision on what you do know. Intuition helps. Your heart often knows more about what's going on than your head!

Hey, I'm Talking to You!

Something told me I shouldn't go down that road, but I did. I stepped small, though, and I thought I'd get by with a few things—little things, really. Like wearing outfits I didn't like, but my boyfriend did. Sporting a hairstyle he thought the epitome of femininity, but I considered a maintenance nightmare.

As I was skipping down the living-to-please-him path, I didn't quite realize the extent of my travels. That is, until I found myself agreeing to a wedding date convenient for him and his work, but terribly inconvenient for me and my schedule. Now there's a biggie for you, and that's when I realized that it was high time to make a U-turn!

I guess most of us start down wrong roads that way—slowly at first, taking baby steps until we look back and realize we're really, really far from home. Perhaps that's when intuition leaps in front of us and shouts, "See, this is what I've been trying to tell you all along!"

My U-turn didn't take me back to where I started, unsure of myself and the validity of my feelings and opinions—but back to being me. A "me" willing to be myself, for better or for worse, and listen for the gentle voice of my heart to guide me forward.

Let us remember that within us there is a palace of immense magnificence.

Teresa of Avila

The work will teach you how to do it.
Proverb

To measure up to all that is demanded
of him, a man must overestimate
his capacities.
Johann Wolfgang von Goethe

I learn by going where I have to go.
Theodore Roethke

What one has to do usually can be done.
Eleanor Roosevelt

There is no instinct like that of the heart.
Lord Byron

When you don't know the whole story...

- Resist the temptation to "fill in the blanks" with fear, hearsay, and suspicion.

- Delay making judgments, choices, and decisions, if at all possible.

- Ask around—you might be surprised at the number of people who have perception, knowledge, and experience, but are hesitant to interfere.

- Trust your gut feelings. Sometimes it's best to run in the opposite direction, no matter what anyone else might think.

Intuition is a whisper of the heart…a silent voice of wisdom deep within the soul. It cautions…are you listening? It warns… do you heed it? It opens the doors of your strength and skills, your abilities and understanding, if you go where it directs.

Intuition is the hunch that compels you to move forward…to take this road over that one…to attempt what you fear. It leads you to try the impossible…to embrace God's blessings…to have faith in yourself.

Intuition protects…trusts…believes.

Whereas the mind works in possibilities,
the intuitions work in actualities,
and what you intuitively desire, that is possible to you.
Whereas what you mentally or "consciously" desire
is nine times out of ten impossible;
hitch your wagon to a star,
or you will just stay where you are.

D. H. Lawrence

You can run...
But you can't hide!

Duck away as we might, but our problems trot right after us! Denial, excuses, escapism—nothing works. So let's wake up and smell the bacon: There's no better way to handle a problem than to turn around and tackle it.

Tackling a problem might mean admitting mistakes or grappling with an uncomfortable reality. It can involve opening a difficult conversation with someone we love. Perhaps the solution requires a major change on our part.

There are lots of reasons to run, but not one of them puts much distance between you and a problem. Sometimes you simply have to go whole hog in dealing with it.

Denial ain't just a river in Egypt.

Mark Twain

All problems become smaller if you don't dodge them, but confront them.

William F. Halsey

It isn't that they can't see the solution, it's that they can't see the problem.

G. K. Chesterton

Outline a problem as clearly as possible and you've already half-solved it.

John Dewey

How to deal with denial...

- Accept unpleasant or unwelcome facts rather than refuse to see them. Facts don't go away simply by turning a blind eye.

- Confront the problem in a timely manner; don't put it off, because the longer it's denied, the harder it is to discuss.

- Examine why you or others are trying to reject the topic. The answer may lie in the emotions, perceptions, customs, and sensitivities involved.

- Weigh the importance of the problem; avoid excuses that would minimize a significant issue, but drop it if it's insignificant.

Problem Solved

Three guys were sitting around boasting about their experiences. One fellow told how he had crawled under a house to retrieve a neighbor's escaped boa constrictor. The next fellow reported that he had once tackled a vicious dog that had a little old lady cornered.

"That's nothing, guys," the third said. "I came face to face with an elephant once, and he was headed right at me!"

"Wow, man," his buddies gasped. "What did you do?"

"Well, I tried standing still and looking him straight in the eye, but he kept coming at me. Then I tried moving backward verrry slowly, but the elephant started moving faster in my direction."

The guys were impressed with his courage. "So how did you finally get away?" they asked.

"I turned around, bought a hot dog, and went to another part of the zoo."

Hidden Blessings

Sometimes there's no way to make the problem smaller. It's huge, life-changing, and beyond anything we feel prepared to take on. Refusing to accept it, however, only brings us another problem—an elephant in the room, and he's not backing away.

Our willingness to approach the issue, take responsibility for our feelings, and remain open, flexible, and teachable helps us come to terms with unwelcome life events. And perhaps, after time and understanding have done their part, we will find a measure of comfort hiding in the shadows.

When you encounter difficulties and contradictions, do not try to break them, but bend them with gentleness and time.

Francis de Sales

Oh, a trouble's a ton, or a trouble's an ounce,
Or a trouble is what you make it,
And it isn't the fact that you're hurt that counts,
But only how did you take it?

Edmund Vance Cooke

Small Bothers, Big Problem

"Doncha wanna play? Huh? Huh?"

If you've ever started a collection, say, of figurines, tea cups, or souvenir spoons, you know how quickly all those little knickknacks fill up a shelf…and then another. The same with annoyances. A little aggravation here, a few pet peeves there, and suddenly you've got a whole new outlook on life—24/7 annoyance.

It's probably okay to keep your stash of spoons (as long as you can keep building shelves), but that annoyance collection has got to go. Even if there are only a few things that bring you daily displeasure, that's a few too many. Just get rid of all of them.

Offense Not Taken

I think I've passed from the Age of Aquarius to the Age of Annoyances. I find them wherever I go—the shriek of kids in crowded shopping malls, the blaring of music in stores, smooth-cheeked gals who don't look a day over 12 selling me wrinkle cream.

And there are scads of irritations right in my own home. How's this for starters: a husband who refuses to pick up his socks. Is the hamper something I keep under lock and key? How about my kids trying to sneak texts to their friends during dinner? Do they think I don't notice that their eyes are fixed on their laps? You get the picture.

One morning I woke up with yesterday's complaints on my mind. Now that made me stop and think. My collection of personal gripes was growing out of control. I expected to be upset when I went out. I expected my husband and kids to do something exasperating. Small annoyances were becoming a big problem, and I was joining the ranks of the perpetually aggrieved.

I decided to go cold turkey on this one—no more griping. No more complaints about things I can't change. It's time to make peace with people as they are and the world as it is. There are too many truly important—and downright delightful—things in life to think about!

A dog that barks all the time gets little attention.

Proverb

Not being able to govern events, I govern myself.

Michel de Montaigne

Wit is the salt of conversation, not the food, and few things in the world are more wearying than a sarcastic attitude towards life.

Agnes Repplier

To hear complaints is wearisome to the wretched and the happy alike.

Samuel Johnson

Now *That's* Annoying!

One morning two hens were pecking in the yard. Suddenly a softball appeared from over the fence and landed with a plop! right next to them. "Well, biddy of a show-off!" one hen gasped to the other. "Look at what she's laying next door!"

Tips to handle all the little (and big) wrinkles in life...

- Love yourself. If you're unhappy with yourself, you'll be unhappy with everyone else.

- Choose to notice other things. Instead of dwelling on what's irritating you, think about something you like.

- Tolerate others. Most often, they're just being themselves and not trying to offend you.

- Listen to others' points of view. Try to understand, even if you don't approve.

- Offer solutions rather than criticisms.

Seek not that the things which happen
should happen as you wish;
but wish the things which happen
to be as they are, and you will have
a tranquil flow of life.

Epictetus

Ahhh!

"Life is good."

Despite everything, life is good. Big issues and major challenges keep us growing; small problems and minor hurdles keep us nimble and attentive. There are enough gentle thoughts, happy memories, uplifting dreams, and peaceful moments to make every day genuine, personal, and real.

Rest in knowing that you have everything you need to deal with the big "bads" in your life and to squash the small "bads." You possess the power to embrace all the good in your life—brilliant, awesome things that make you say "wow!" and tiny fragile things that draw contented sighs and gentle smiles.

Serenity. That's it. Yes, life is good.

Start by doing what's necessary;
then do what's possible;
and suddenly you are doing the impossible.
Francis of Assisi